11/5/14

STRANDED!
Testing the Limits of Survival

Lost at SEA

by G. S. Prentzas

Consultant: Bob Cooper
Australian Survival Expert

BEARPORT
PUBLISHING

New York, New York

Credits

Cover, © Chad Zuber/Shutterstock, © Pavel L Photo and Video/Shutterstock, and © Computer Earth/Shutterstock; 4BL, © AP Images; 4–5, © Wikipedia; 5C, © AP Images; 6C, © Bike Rider London/Shutterstock; 7, © E. G. Pors/Shutterstock; 8B, © Dive–Hive/Shutterstock; 9T, © AP Images; 9B, © Stanalex/Shutterstock; 10, © Jeff Rottman/Photolibrary/Getty Images; 11, © Dirschert Reinhard/Prisma/Superstock; 12BL, © Damerau/Shutterstock; 12–13, © Pavel Vakhrushev/Shutterstock; 13BL, © Philip Stephen/Nature PL/Corbis; 14C, © Steven Callahan; 14BR, © AP Images; 15, © Stefan Pircher/Shutterstock; 16, © Joe Quinn/Alamy; 17, © AP Images; 18, © Steven Callahan; 19CR, © Wikipedia; 19B, © Zerosub/Shutterstock; 20, © Design Pics/Thinkstock; 20BR, © Outdoor-Archiv/Alamy; 21, © Steven Callahan; 22, © Brett Archibald; 24B, © Brett Archibald; 25B, © Brett Archibald; 25CR, © Brett Archibald; 26, © Brett Archibald; 27, © Barry Hall, Deputy Launch Authority St. Ives Lifeboat Station; 28, © Wikipedia; 29, © Kaschibo/Shutterstock.

Publisher: Kenn Goin
Senior Editor: Joyce Tavolacci
Creative Director: Spencer Brinker
Photo Research: Brown Bear Books Ltd

Library of Congress Cataloging-in-Publication Data

Prentzas, G. S.
 Lost at sea / by G. S. Prentzas.
    pages cm — (Stranded! Testing the limits of survival)
 Includes bibliographical references and index.
 ISBN-13: 978-1-62724-290-5 (library binding)
 ISBN-10: 1-62724-290-2 (library binding)
 1. Marine accidents—Juvenile literature. 2. Survival at sea—Juvenile literature. 3. Sailors—Biography—Juvenile literature. I. Title.
 G525.P75 2015
 910.4'52—dc23
                                        2014004640

For more information, write to Bearport Publishing Company, Inc., 45 West 21st Street, Suite 3B, New York, New York 10010. Printed in the United States of America.

10 9 8 7 6 5 4 3 2 1

Contents

Gone Fishing

On a windy morning in April 2005, two friends went fishing near Charleston, South Carolina. Teenagers Troy Driscoll and Josh Long paddled their small 15-foot (4.6 m) boat into the rough Atlantic Ocean. They planned to stay close to shore and fish for only a few hours.

Troy and Josh paddled out into the Atlantic Ocean from this beach on Sullivan's Island, South Carolina.

On the day the two teens went fishing, **forecasters** warned boaters about high winds and rough seas.

Troy Driscoll (left) and
Josh Long (right)

Not long after setting out, their boat became caught in a powerful **rip current**. It began to sweep the small **vessel** away from shore. The frightened teenagers tried paddling back to land with all their might, but the current was too strong. It pushed their boat farther and farther into deeper water. Troy and Josh soon lost sight of land. They had no food or water and no radio to call for help. "We knew we were in trouble," said Josh.

Troy and Josh's small boat, shown here, had no sail or motor. This made it especially hard for the boys to move and control their boat.

Waiting For Help

As night fell, it became very cold. The friends huddled together to stay warm. Eight-foot (2.4 m) waves pounded their boat, showering the teenagers with chilly water. In the morning, the cold, exhausted boys hoped that help would come. They looked for ships passing by. Finally, they spotted some fishing boats in the distance. Troy and Josh **frantically** waved their arms in the air. However, the fishermen didn't see them in the **vast** ocean.

For extra warmth, Troy and Josh shared a two-piece wet suit that they found in the boat. One boy wore the top, and the other boy wore the bottom.

A wet suit keeps a person's body warm in cold water and in cold air.

Several days passed as Troy and Josh's boat continued to **drift**. One night, the boys were startled awake by a deep roar. As they glanced up, they saw a huge container ship several stories high pass within ten feet (3 m) of their boat! Unfortunately, it was too dark for the ship's crew to see them. The enormous ship sped past them, creating a giant wave that almost **capsized** their tiny vessel and nearly tossed the boys into the water.

A container ship like the one that almost slammed into Troy and Josh's boat

Fighting to Survive

Without water and food, Troy and Josh became incredibly thirsty and hungry. **Desperate** to drink, they slurped up rainwater that collected at the bottom of their boat. The boys faced another serious problem—no shelter. During the day, the hot sun baked their skin. To cool off, the teenagers took short swims in the cold ocean water. One boy swam, while the other watched for sharks.

Even though there's a lot of water in the ocean, it's salty. Drinking seawater will make a person very sick—and can even cause death.

Sharks live throughout the world's oceans. They do not normally attack people but will sometimes do so if they mistake a person for a seal or large fish.

Finally, after more than six days at sea, a passing fishing boat spotted and rescued the teens. Doctors treated them for **dehydration** and bad sunburns. Despite the terrible experience, Troy and Josh said they would go boating again. Next time, however, they would take a boat with a motor!

Josh Long rests in a hospital after being rescued.

Troy and Josh were rescued by a fishing boat like this one.

The World's Oceans

As Troy and Josh discovered, it's easy to become lost in the ocean. Why? Oceans are vast bodies of salt water. They are so big that many parts of them can be thousands of miles from land, making it difficult to find people who are lost at sea. Oceans can also be tens of thousands of feet deep.

Earth has five huge oceans that cover more than two-thirds of the planet's surface.

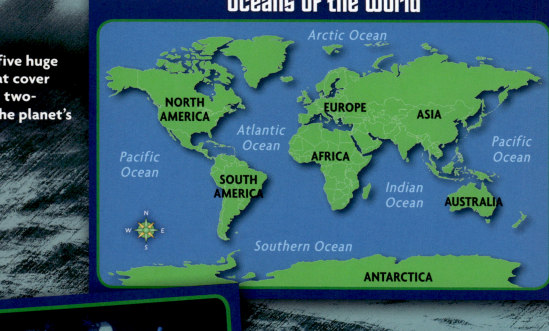

Oceans of the World

Arctic Ocean

NORTH AMERICA

EUROPE

ASIA

Atlantic Ocean

Pacific Ocean

AFRICA

SOUTH AMERICA

Indian Ocean

Pacific Ocean

AUSTRALIA

Southern Ocean

ANTARCTICA

This deep-sea submarine is exploring the Pacific Ocean.

The deepest part of the ocean is called the Challenger Deep in the Pacific Ocean. It's about 36,200 feet (11,034 m) deep.

Oceans are home to more than a million kinds of plants and animals, all of which are perfectly suited to life at sea. For example, seals can hold their breath for up to an hour and dive up to 5,000 feet (1,525 m) to catch their food. Whales have a thick layer of fat called blubber that helps keep them warm in deep, cold ocean waters.

Sperm whales dive into the cold ocean depths.

Dangers at Sea

Although many plants and animals thrive in the ocean, people who are lost at sea struggle to survive. One of the main reasons is that even though oceans have lots of water, people can't drink it because it's so salty. As a result, many people who are lost at sea often die from lack of water.

Finding food on the open seas is another challenge. Why? People **adrift** in the ocean often don't have the tools needed to hunt for fish and other sea animals. Without the right kind of equipment, they can starve.

One of the only animals that can drink salt water without getting sick is a bird called an albatross.

Each gallon (3.8 l) of ocean water contains about eight ounces (227 g) of salt. That's about 48 teaspoons!

Fierce storms and extreme weather add to the danger of the sea. Monster waves and strong winds can knock over boats and sink them. People who are adrift have little or no protection on the open seas. The blazing sun can dehydrate a person and burn his or her skin. Freezing cold weather can lead to **hypothermia**—and even death. A person lost at sea must be good at quickly solving problems to stay alive. That's exactly what sailor Steve Callahan did after he was shipwrecked in the Atlantic Ocean.

Rough seas crash against a fishing boat in the North Atlantic.

A Jolt in the Night

In January 1982, Steve Callahan set sail from the Canary Islands, located off Africa's northwest coast. He planned to sail across the Atlantic Ocean and arrive in Antigua, a small island in the Caribbean Sea, entirely on his own. That's a distance of nearly 3,000 miles (4,828 km).

Steve's boat, the *Napoleon Solo*

Steve Callahan

About a week into his trip, on a moonlit night, Steve was abruptly awakened by a loud bang. Something had crashed into his boat, poking a hole in its side. Thousands of gallons of cold water gushed in as the boat began to sink. "This is it," Steve remembers thinking. "I'm going to die." Steve knew if he didn't snap into action immediately, he'd drown. So he quickly **inflated** a tiny, five-foot (1.5 m) life raft and tied it to the sailboat to keep it from floating away. An experienced sailor, Steve knew he needed much more than a rubber raft and the small amount of supplies in it, however, if he were to survive at sea.

A large shark, such as this great white, might have hit and made a big hole in Steve's boat.

Steve Callahan believes a whale or shark struck his boat, causing it to sink.

Alone in a Raft

Steve remembered he had stored food and other supplies in the sailboat's **cabin**, which was now filling up with water. He dove into the chilly water and swam into the cabin. "I held my breath and went under again and again." Steve grabbed a sleeping bag, food, and an **emergency survival kit**. He dragged the supplies back to the raft.

A sailboat, similar to Steve's, fills with water and sinks into the sea.

As Steve crawled into the raft to rest, the seas became rough. Ten-foot (3 m) waves crashed around him. Then the rope connecting the raft to his flooded boat came loose. Waves swept the raft away from his sinking sailboat. Steve was now alone on a tiny raft in the middle of the ocean. He would have to find a way to stay alive until help arrived, but how?

A life raft, much like the one Steve was on, bobs in the vast Atlantic Ocean.

When Steve was shipwrecked, he was about 2,071 miles (3,333 km) from the nearest land.

Food and Water

Adrift in his raft, Steve worried about how he would survive at sea. He had little food, just an egg, a can of beans, cabbage, and some peanuts, and only about a gallon (3.8 l) of water. He knew that would keep him alive for less than two weeks. To survive longer than that, Steve would need to figure out how to get more food and water.

Steve used a handmade tool to help him figure out in what direction his raft was floating.

Steve soon noticed fish, including dorados and triggerfish, swimming near his life raft. Luckily, he had stashed a speargun in the raft. Steve used it to catch fish, and he even caught a few seabirds that landed on the raft. He gobbled them down raw. For water, he found three **stills** in his emergency survival kit. He used the stills to remove salt from the seawater so he could drink it. "Even at that," he says, "I was thirsty all the time." Without the stills, however, Steve would have died quickly from dehydration.

The stills that Steve used, similar to this one, made about 16 ounces (0.5 l) of water a day—or about two glasses.

A dorado is one of the kinds of fish Steve hunted with his speargun.

Fish gathered in the shade under Steve's raft. This made it easier for Steve to catch them.

Hope Fades

After weeks without enough food and water, Steve became weak and struggled to stay alert. Food and water weren't his only worries, however. Waves crashed against the raft. Salt water caused his skin to **blister** and created open wounds. In addition, the raft had sprung leaks, requiring frequent repairs. After many weeks at sea, "I had no more to give," Steve said. Somehow, however, he found the strength to push on.

Waves drenched Steve's raft and body with seawater.

Moist skin can easily blister, leading to severe discomfort.

On the night of April 20, 1982, after drifting for 75 days, Steve finally spotted a lighthouse! The next day, a fishing boat from the Caribbean island of Marie-Galante approached his raft. Fishermen had seen birds circling offshore and believed they were feeding on fish. The men sped out in their boat, hoping to catch the fish. The fishermen discovered the birds and fish around Steve's life raft and rescued him.

Steve lost a third of his body weight while lost at sea for 76 days. It took him six months to fully recover.

Steve's Journey Across the Atlantic

Canary Islands

Atlantic Ocean

Antigua

AFRICA

Marie-Galante

SOUTH AMERICA

N W E S

Steve (second from left) poses with the fishermen who rescued him.

After Steve's sailboat sank, he drifted more than 2,000 miles (3,219 km) across the Atlantic in a life raft until he was rescued near the island of Marie-Galante.

A Surfing Vacation

Steve Callahan struggled to survive while lost at sea, even with a raft and supplies. Brett Archibald faced a more serious situation while vacationing on the island of Sumatra in Indonesia in 2013.

On April 16, the 50-year-old surfer took an overnight boat trip to a nearby island to go surfing. At about 3:00 a.m., Brett became **seasick** and climbed up to the boat's **deck** for some fresh air. Once on the deck, Brett became dizzy and tumbled overboard into the dark water below.

Brett Archibald
surfing in Indonesia

Indonesia is a country between the Pacific Ocean and the Indian Ocean that is made up of more than 17,500 islands.

"I don't remember falling overboard," said Brett. "But I woke up in the water with no life jacket." Brett screamed for help, but no one heard him. Then he watched helplessly as the boat sailed away—without him. When Brett did not show up for breakfast that morning, the ship's crew knew something was wrong. They alerted rescuers, who began searching for Brett.

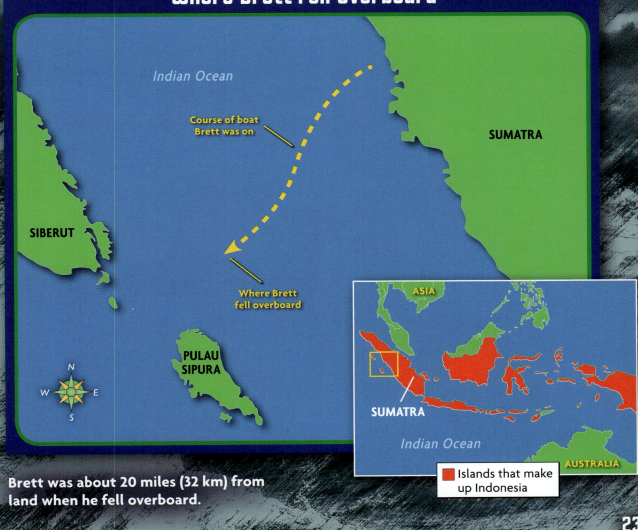

Where Brett Fell Overboard

Indian Ocean

Course of boat Brett was on

SUMATRA

SIBERUT

Where Brett fell overboard

N
W   E
S

PULAU SIPURA

ASIA

SUMATRA

Indian Ocean

AUSTRALIA

Islands that make up Indonesia

Brett was about 20 miles (32 km) from land when he fell overboard.

Staying Afloat

To stay alive, Brett began **treading water**. He soon became tired and switched to floating on his back. During the night, Brett nearly drowned as he struggled to keep his head above water. He faced additional dangers as well. "I had sharks swimming past me. I got stung by a jellyfish," he said. The worst attacks came from seagulls. They tried to peck Brett's eyes out and left two big bloody holes near his nose.

A man practices floating on his back, the same method Brett used to survive at sea.

Brett began losing hope. Somehow, however, he gained the strength to keep treading. About 6:30 a.m., 27 hours after Brett fell overboard, a ship spotted him. "I'd never been so happy to see a boat in my entire life," said Brett. The crew pulled him from the water and brought him to shore. He was tired, sunburned, hungry, and thirsty, but his spirits remained high. "We've had a good adventure," Brett said, just after he was rescued.

The crew of the *Barrenjoey* spotted and rescued Brett.

Brett being rescued

Brett Archibald was rescued about 12 miles (19 km) from where he had fallen into the water.

Making It Back to Land

Brett Archibald found out the hard way just how dangerous the ocean can be. Despite the hardships he faced, Brett fully recovered from his ordeal. "The human body is an amazing, amazing thing," Brett said. In a phone call home to his family, Brett told his wife that he wanted to continue his surfing vacation. "We've got eight days left on our trip, I can't go to the hospital, we've got to surf!" he said to her.

Brett Archibald reunited with his family after his frightening adventure at sea.

Steve Callahan felt that his experience of being lost at sea made him enjoy life more. That's not all he gained from the unexpected and dangerous experience, however. Like others who have returned from being lost at sea, he has learned that the key to survival at sea is to remain calm, to make smart decisions, and to never give up. "But would I want to be adrift in the ocean again?" he said. "No way."

A rescue crew tows a disabled boat back to shore near Saint Ives, England.

Rescuers use ships, small airplanes, and helicopters to search for and help people lost at sea.

Ocean Survival Tips

If you plan on going out on the ocean, follow these tips to help you survive.

☑ Make sure your boat is equipped with emergency gear. A life raft, life jackets, **flares**, two-way radio, first-aid kit, and solar water stills are essential.

☑ Tell people in advance where you are traveling and when you plan to return.

☑ Take bottled water, canned or dried food, sunscreen, and fishing gear.

☑ Never drink salt water. It will make you sick and dehydrated. Your body needs at least two cups (0.5 l) of fresh water to flush out every cup (0.2 l) of salt water you drink.

☑ Do not expect to be rescued quickly. **Ration** water and food supplies.

A life raft should be large enough to hold emergency supplies, including food, water, life jackets, and a radio to call for help.

Use **tarps** and containers to collect rainwater to drink.

 Use clothes, tarps, mats or blankets, and even seaweed to protect yourself from the sun and wind. Wind and heat from the sun can make you dehydrated and burn, blister, and crack your skin.

✔ Stay dry. Salt water can dry out your skin and cause sores.

✔ Prevent hypothermia by covering your head, arms, and legs. Doing this will keep your body from losing heat.

✔ Stay out of the water. Sharks, barracuda, jellyfish, and other sea creatures can injure or harm you.

A barracuda has sharp teeth and can bite.

Glossary

adrift (uh-DRIFT) floating freely through the water

blister (BLISS-tur) to form swellings on the surface of the skin

cabin (KAB-in) the living area inside a boat

capsized (KAP-syezd) turned over in the water

deck (DEK) a platform that forms the floor of a boat or ship

dehydration (*dee*-hye-DRAY-shuhn) the condition of not having enough water in a one's body

desperate (DESS-pur-it) willing to do anything to fix an urgent situation

drift (DRIFT) to be carried along by water or wind

emergency survival kit (i-MUR-juhn-see sur-VIVE-uhl KIT) a set of equipment needed to stay alive after a dangerous event

flares (FLAIRZ) devices that burst into flames to signal rescuers

forecasters (FOR-kast-urz) people who predict what the weather will be in the future

frantically (FRAN-tik-lee) to do something with worry or fear

hypothermia (*hye*-puh-THUR-mee-uh) a condition in which a person's body temperature becomes dangerously low

inflated (in-FLAY-tuhd) blew up with air

ration (RASH-uhn) to use in small amounts to save resources

rip current (RIP KUR-uhnt) water within the ocean that moves quickly away from shore

seasick (SEE-*sik*) feeling ill because of the movement of a boat or waves

stills (STILLS) devices that use heat from the sun to make drinking water from salt water

tarps (TARPS) heavy coverings

treading water (TRED-ing WAH-tur) remaining afloat in water by moving one's legs and arms

vast (VAST) huge in area

vessel (VESS-uhl) a ship or boat

Bibliography

Callahan, Steven. *Adrift: Seventy-Six Days Lost at Sea.* Boston: Houghton Mifflin (1986).

Herreshoff, Halsey C. *The Sailor's Handbook.* Camden, ME: International Marine/McGraw-Hill (2006).

Wiseman, John 'Lofty'. *SAS Survival Handbook: For Any Climate, In Any Situation.* New York: HarperCollins (2009).

Read More

Buchholz, Rachel. *How to Survive Anything.* Washington, D.C.: National Geographic (2011).

MacQuitty, Miranda. *Ocean (Eyewitness Books).* New York: DK (2008).

O'Shei, Tim. *How to Survive Being Lost at Sea (Prepare to Survive).* North Mankato, MN: Capstone (2009).

Learn More Online

To learn more about surviving at sea, visit
www.bearportpublishing.com/Stranded!

Index

About the Author

*G. S. Prentzas has written more than 30 books for young readers.
He enjoys sea kayaking and is happy never to have been lost at sea.*